Smithsonian

The Secrets of NEPTUNE

by Thomas K. Adamson

CAPSTONE PRESS
a capstone imprint

Capstone Press
1710 Roe Crest Drive, North Mankato, Minnesota 56003
www.capstonepub.com

Library of Congress Cataloging-in-Publication Data
Adamson, Thomas K.—author.
  The secrets of Neptune / by Thomas K. Adamson.
    pages cm. — (Smithsonian. Planets)
  Summary: "Discusses the planet Neptune, including observations by ancient cultures, current knowledge of Neptune,
and plans for future scientific research and space exploration"—Provided by publisher.
  Audience: Ages 8-10
  Audience: Grades 2 to 4
  ISBN 978-1-4914-5867-9 (library binding)
  ISBN 978-1-4914-5900-3 (paperback)
  ISBN 978-1-4914-5911-9 (eBook PDF)
1. Neptune (Planet)—Juvenile literature. 2. Neptune (Planet)—Exploration—Juvenile literature. I. Title.
  QB691.A34 2016
  523.48—dc23   2014046200

Editorial Credits
Elizabeth R. Johnson, editor; Tracy Davies McCabe and Kazuko Collins, designers;
Wanda Winch, media researcher; Tori Abraham, production specialist

Our very special thanks to Andrew K. Johnston, Geographer, Center for Earth and Planetary Studies, National Air and Space Museum,
Smithsonian Institution, for his curatorial review. Capstone would also like to thank Kealy Gordon, Smithsonian Institution Product
Development Manager, and the following at Smithsonian Enterprises: Ellen Nanney, Licensing Manager; Brigid Ferraro, Director of Licensing;
Carol LeBlanc, Senior Vice President, Consumer & Education Products; Chris Liedel, President.

Photo Credits
Black Cat Studios: Ron Miller, 15, 18, 23; Courtesy of Dr. Heidi Hammel, 28; Courtesy of Smithsonian Institution Libraries, Washington, DC:
Dibner Library of the History of Science and Technology, 7 (bottom left); Don Davis, 22; Getty Images: Hulton Archives/Space Frontiers,
12; Lunar and Planetary Institute, 5 (bottom); NASA: Johnson Space Center, 27, ESA/Hubble Heritage Team (StScl/AURA), 13, JPL, cover,
back cover, 1, 5 (back), 16, 17, JPL/USGS, 19, JPL-Caltech, 26; Newscom: akg-images, 7 (right); Rijksmuseum, Amsterdam, 8; Science Source:
Detlev van Ravenswaay, 9, John R. Foster, 25, Royal Institution of Great Britain, 7 (top left), Walter Myers, 21; Shutterstock: bluecrayola, 29,
photoplotnikov, 11, Tjeffersion, space background

Direct Quotations
Page 28 from the September 1, 2008, New York Times interview with Heidi Hammel, www.nytimes.com

Printed in Canada.
032015   008825FRF15

Table of Contents

Disappearing Dark Spot

When the Voyager 2 robotic spacecraft flew by Neptune in 1989, it gave us our first close look at the eighth planet. Scientists were amazed at Neptune's beautiful blue color. They were surprised to find it had a huge dark spot.

Five years later the Hubble Space Telescope took pictures of Neptune. The Dark Spot was gone. What happened to it? Do spots come and go that quickly on Neptune? It's one of Neptune's secrets that scientists are still studying.

Neptune is almost 4 times wider than Earth. If Earth were as wide as a dime, Neptune would be a baseball.

Fast Facts

Distance from Sun: 2.8 billion miles (4.5 billion kilometers)

Diameter: 30,599 miles (49,244 km)

Moons: 13 (and likely one more)

Rings: 5

Length of day: 16 hours

Length of year: 165 Earth years

Earth

Neptune

Discovery of Neptune

Ancient cultures did not know about Neptune. The planet can only be seen with a telescope. Neptune was not discovered until 1846.

The first hints of Neptune's existence actually came from an observation of the planet's neighbor, Uranus. Astronomers had seen that the pattern of Uranus' orbit was not what it should be. They thought there might be another planet nearby causing the unusual orbit.

Two mathematicians worked out the calculations to explain the differences. John Couch Adams of England and Urbain Le Verrier of France predicted the location of the suspected planet. They each figured out the same thing independently. A year later, in 1846, Astronomer Johann Galle spotted Neptune with a telescope using their predictions.

Neptune is the first planet found by mathematical calculations.

John Couch Adams

Urbain Le Verrier

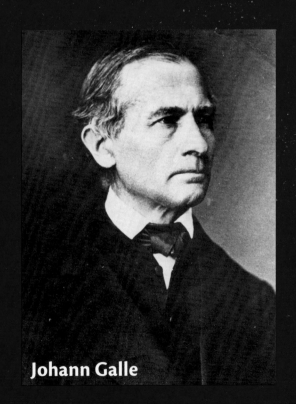

Johann Galle

Galle wanted to name the new planet Le Verrier, after the man who sent him the calculations. But all other planets are named for Greek and Roman gods from mythology.

The planet appeared blue in telescopes and reminded people of the blue color of the sea. So Le Verrier instead named it Neptune, after the Roman god of the sea.

Neptune

Galileo Galilei discovered Jupiter's moons in 1610. He saw Neptune with his telescope in 1613 but did not realize it was a planet. He recorded it as a star.

Galle spotted Neptune on September 23, 1846. British astronomer William Lassell discovered Neptune's largest moon, Triton, just 17 days later.

Celestial Mechanics

Celestial mechanics is a branch of astronomy that studies the movements of celestial objects, like planets, moons, asteroids, and stars, and the way they interact with one another. The discovery of Neptune, using mathematical calculations, was proof that celestial mechanics was an important field of study.

An Atmosphere of Ice and Gas

Like the other giant planets, such as Jupiter and Saturn, Neptune has no solid surface. Jupiter and Saturn are called gas giants. They are made of mostly gas. Neptune is also mostly gas, but because it's so far away from the Sun, the gases are icy. Neptune is a gas giant and also an ice giant.

Neptune's atmosphere is made up of hydrogen, helium, and methane. The atmosphere gets thicker deep within the planet. The icy gases gradually melt into liquids. Neptune possibly has a solid core the size of Earth.

The methane gas in the atmosphere causes Neptune's blue color. Methane absorbs red light from the Sun and reflects blue light. Neptune has slightly more methane than Uranus, giving it a deeper blue than Uranus.

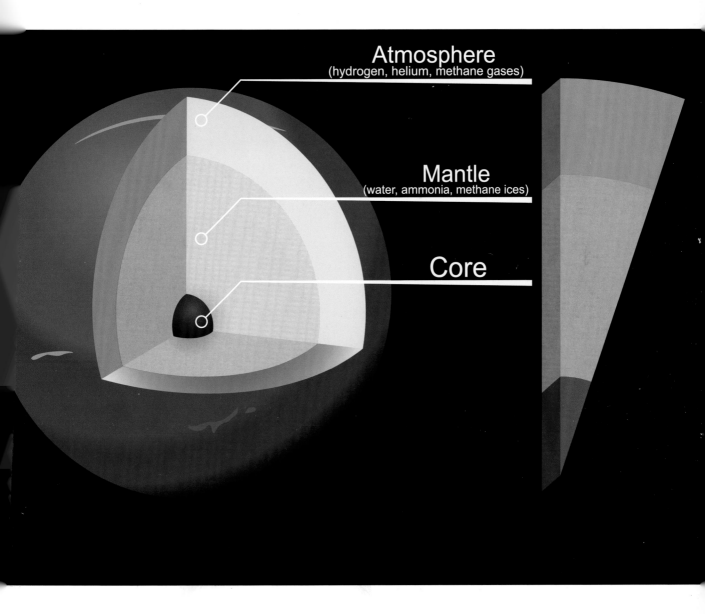

Atmosphere
(hydrogen, helium, methane gases)

Mantle
(water, ammonia, methane ices)

Core

Methane is a colorless, odorless gas. Methane is in the atmospheres of all the giant planets. It is also found in Earth's atmosphere, but in a much smaller amount.

A Stormy Planet

When Voyager 2 flew by Neptune in 1989, its pictures showed a huge dark storm bigger than Earth. Scientists named it the Great Dark Spot. It looked like Jupiter's famous Great Red Spot, which has been storming for hundreds of years.

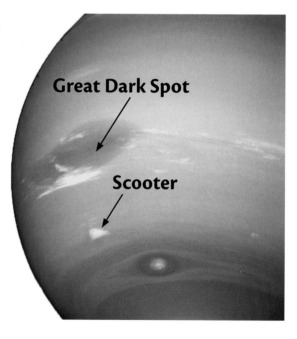

Great Dark Spot

Scooter

The Hubble Space Telescope observed Neptune in 1994. The Great Dark Spot was nowhere in sight. How could something so huge disappear so quickly? Not only that, but now a different large storm had mysteriously appeared.

Storms on Neptune seem to appear and disappear within only a few years. Scientists are not sure why Neptune is so stormy. Heat created inside the planet could be causing the storms. But Neptune's stormy weather is still one of the planet's big secrets.

Another spot seen in Voyager 2 pictures was called Scooter because it moved so fast around the planet.

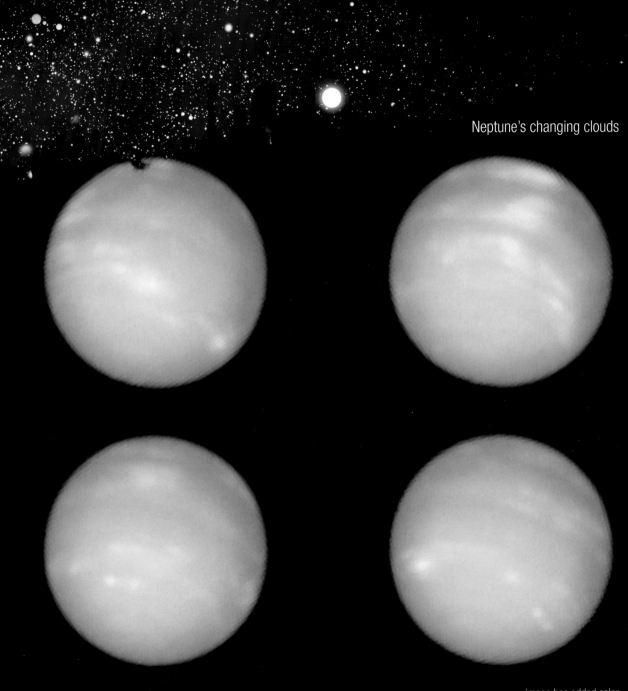

Neptune's changing clouds

image has added color

Scientists planned the Voyager 2 launch for a time
when all the giant planets were lined up. This allowed
the spacecraft to fly by all four of them in one long trip.

Cold Clouds

Bright white clouds float around the top of Neptune's atmosphere. The wispy clouds are frozen methane. These high altitude clouds are about 35 miles (56 km) above the cloud layers below. Scientists can tell this distance because of the shadows the clouds cast.

Temperatures in these cloud tops are -353 degrees Fahrenheit (-214 °Celsius), far colder than any weather on Earth. But something inside Neptune is producing heat. Otherwise, these clouds would be even colder. Scientists are not sure what is making this heat.

artist illustration of Neptune's atmosphere

Neptune is the windiest place in the solar system. Winds on Neptune can blow more than 1,300 miles (2,100 km) per hour. That's almost twice the speed of sound on Earth.

15

Voyager 2

Voyager 2 is the only spacecraft that has visited Neptune. Launched in 1977, its mission was to fly past all of the giant planets. Before it flew past Neptune in 1989, Voyager 2 took close-up photos of Jupiter, Saturn, and Uranus.

After Voyager 2 flew past Neptune, it kept going. It still sends signals to Earth, even though it is done taking pictures. The signals give scientists clues about what the outer reaches of the solar system are like. Voyager 2 has enough power to last until about 2025. It will then be unable to send signals. But it will continue drifting into the space between the stars.

Voyager 2 carries a special message for any extraterrestrials that might find the spacecraft far into the future. The Golden Record shares photos and sound recordings from Earth. These symbols give instructions for how to play the record and how to find our solar system.

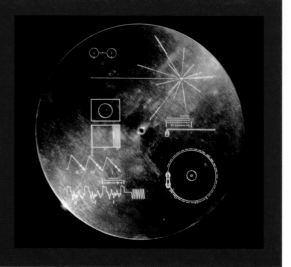

Voyager 2 is about 10 billion miles
(16 billion km) from Earth.

Strange Moon

Voyager 2 did more than take great pictures of Neptune. It took the first close-up pictures of Triton, Neptune's large moon. Triton is Neptune's only large moon as well as its only round moon.

artist illustration of view from Triton

Triton is large enough that the strength of its gravity pulled it into a round shape. Neptune's other moons are much smaller. They have varying shapes, but none of them are round.

cantaloupe texture

polar ice cap

The Voyager 2 photos surprised scientists. Part of Triton looks like a cantaloupe. A pink polar ice cap covers a large part of the moon. Scientists also spotted geysers spewing carbon and nitrogen 10 miles (16 km) above Triton's surface. The material blows across the surface and leaves dark streaks. Scientists didn't expect something in the cold outer solar system to be this active.

Triton is a strange moon for another reason. Its orbit around Neptune is retrograde, or backwards. Triton travels around Neptune the opposite way that Neptune rotates. No other planet's large moons do this.

Triton could have formed somewhere else in the solar system, and as it traveled through space it could have been captured by Neptune's gravity. It's possible that Triton came from the Kuiper Belt before entering into Neptune's orbit. The Kuiper Belt is a region of the solar system beyond Neptune. It is made up of icy objects, including dwarf planets.

Scientists wonder if the dwarf planet Pluto might look like Triton. The New Horizons spacecraft flew by Pluto in 2015. Scientists are using the data gathered to find out if Triton and Pluto have similarities.

Triton is probably the coldest large object in the solar system. At -400 °F (-240 °C), it's colder than any place spacecraft have visited.

In Greek mythology,
Triton was Neptune's son.

Small and Hidden Moons

Besides Triton, Neptune has 13 other much smaller moons. These small moons might have formed long ago when larger moons smashed into one another. Proteus is the largest of the small moons. It's one of the darkest objects in the solar system. Proteus probably has less ice and more non-reflective material on its surface than the other moons.

Proteus •

Larissa •
Galatea •

Despina •
Thalassa •
Naiad •

A moon is a natural satellite of a planet. Moons can be round or oddly shaped. They can be created at the same time as the planet, or they can be captured by the planet's gravity at any time. Some asteroids and dwarf planets have natural satellites, and those are called moons too.

Neptune

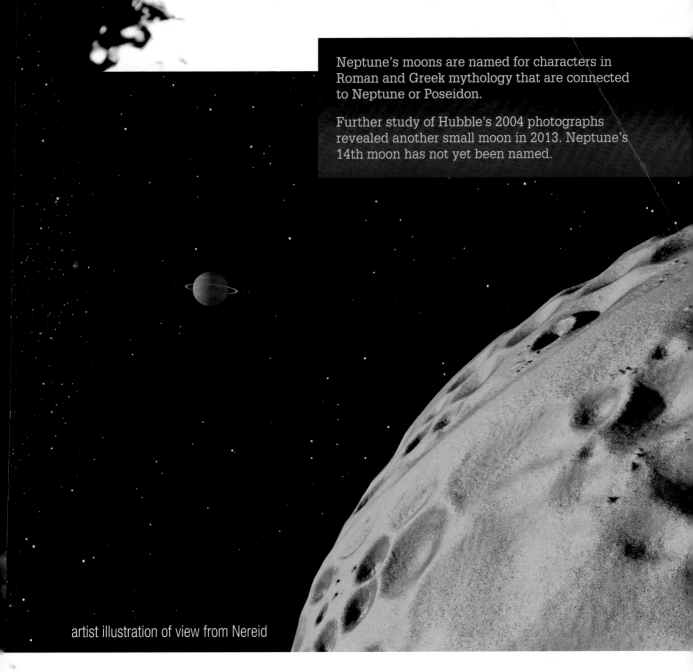

Neptune's moons are named for characters in Roman and Greek mythology that are connected to Neptune or Poseidon.

Further study of Hubble's 2004 photographs revealed another small moon in 2013. Neptune's 14th moon has not yet been named.

artist illustration of view from Nereid

Nereid has the most stretched-out orbit of any planet's moon. Its distance from Neptune changes by about 5 million miles (8 million km) over the course of its orbit. Nereid might also be an object captured by Neptune's gravity.

Rings: Going, Going, Gone?

Like the other giant planets, Neptune has rings. But unlike Saturn's rings, Neptune's are very thin and faint. The outer ring is not even a complete ring. It is made up of three main ring arcs.

Neptune's rings could be the remains of moons that crashed into each other. The rings have changed since Voyager 2's flyby. All of the rings are getting thinner, and scientists think they may disappear completely someday.

Small moons orbit within the rings. The weak gravity of the moons is likely holding the rings together. They are called shepherd moons.

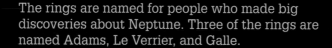

The rings are named for people who made big discoveries about Neptune. Three of the rings are named Adams, Le Verrier, and Galle.

artist illustration of Neptune's rings and moons

Exploring Neptune

There are no planned space missions to Neptune. A mission to the eighth planet would be very expensive. Scientists have to choose missions that could provide the best discoveries for the money spent.

Voyager 2 took 12 years to get to Neptune. We have better technology now than in the 1970s and 1980s. The New Horizons spacecraft traveled for about 9 years before reaching Pluto. A similar spacecraft could reach Neptune in about that much time.

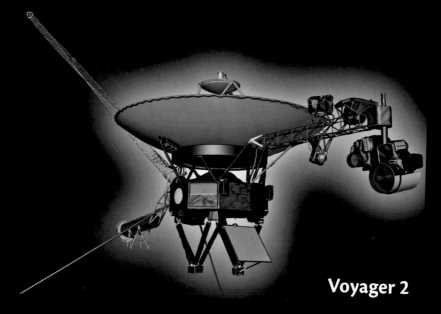

Voyager 2

Hubble Space Telescope

NASA launched the Hubble Space Telescope into Earth's orbit in 1990. Earth's atmosphere changes and blocks the light that reaches our planet. In orbit, Hubble doesn't have to look through the atmosphere and has a much better view of space. Hubble has sent hundreds of thousands of images back to Earth.

Hubble

For now scientists use powerful telescopes to study Neptune. Even from Earth, they can see changes in Neptune's storms.

Scientist Spotlight: Heidi Hammel

Heidi Hammel was on the Voyager 2 science team when the spacecraft flew by Neptune. She now studies the ice giants Uranus and Neptune with Hubble and other telescopes. She says that studying Neptune and Uranus is interesting because they change more than people once thought. She added, "They've been less studied than nearer planets. So whenever I make an observation, anything I find is brand new." Hammel is the Executive Vice President of AURA, the Association of Universities for Research in Astronomy. She is also on the team that is developing the new Webb Telescope.

Scientists are certainly curious to unlock more of Neptune's secrets. They want to learn more about Triton and how active the rest of its surface might be. They want to find out more about Neptune's clouds and storms. Someday a spacecraft will go back to Neptune.

The Great Dark Spot is gone. But the picture of Neptune we see most often is Voyager 2's famous shot of blue Neptune with that spot. How will the next spacecraft's photos of Neptune look?

Glossary

altitude (AL-tih-tood)—the height of something above the ground

arc (AHRK)—part of a curve

astronomy (uh-STRAH-nuh-mee)—the study of stars, planets, and space

atmosphere (AT-muhss-fihr)—the mixture of gases that surrounds a planet or moon

diameter (dye-AM-uh-tur)—a straight line through the center of a circle, from one side to another

dwarf planet (DWORF)—a large, roundish body that orbits the Sun, but is not big enough to disturb other objects from its orbit, and is not a moon

equator (ee-KWAY-tuhr)—an imaginary line around the middle of a planet that is an equal distance from its north and south poles

geyser (GYE-zur)—an underground spring that shoots water, steam, or other material into the air

gravity (GRAV-uh-tee)—the force that pulls things down or to the center of a planet and keeps them from floating away into space

mythology (mih-THAH-luh-jee)—a group of myths or stories that belong to a culture

orbit (OR-bit)—the invisible path followed by an object circling a planet, the Sun, etc.

polar ice cap (POH-lur)—a mound of ice that covers an area of land and gets bigger as snow falls, melts, and freezes, located in the region around the north or south pole

robot (ROH-bot)—a machine that is programmed to do jobs that are usually performed by a person

satellite (SAT-uh-lite)—an object, natural or man-made, orbiting a planet or a moon

Read More

Chiger, Arielle, and Elkin, Matthew. *20 Fun Facts about Gas Giants.* Fun Fact File: Space! New York: Gareth Stevens, 2015.

Owen, Ruth. *Neptune.* Explore Outer Space. New York: Windmill Books, 2014.

Squire, Ann. *Planet Neptune.* A True Book. New York: Children's Press, 2014.

Internet Sites

FactHound offers a safe, fun way to find Internet sites related to this book. All of the sites on FactHound have been researched by our staff.

Here's all you do:

Visit *www.facthound.com*

Type in this code: 9781491458679

FactHound will fetch the best sites for you!

 Check out projects, games and lots more at **www.capstonekids.com**

Critical Thinking Using the Common Core

1. Read the text on page 12. Why were scientists surprised that the Great Dark Spot disappeared? (Key Ideas and Details)

2. Read the text and look at the images on pages 16 and 17. What was Voyager 2's mission? Is the mission completed? Why or why not? (Integration of Knowledge and Ideas)

Index